LIGHT FOR THE BURNING SOUL

Sparks, Flames, and Embers

Lois J. Funk

RIT Publishing
Central Illinois, U.S.A.

Copyright © 2015 Lois J. Funk

ISBN: 978 0692363829

Library of Congress Control Number: 2015930247

Limited edition. All rights reserved. No part of this publication may be reproduced or transmitted in any form or by any means, electronic or mechanical, including photocopying.

Cover Photo Copyright © 2015 Ed Gaitros

Edited by Barbara Pappan

Printed in the United States of America

To the One Who puts
the *Son*light in my soul …

ACKNOWLEDGEMENTS

"Excess Baggage" *The Touch of the Master's Hand*, 1997
"Listen ..." *Poets' Gold*, 1990
"One Life to Give" *Peoria Poetry Club Christmas*, 1989
"Room for One More" *purpose*, 1995; *The Lutheran Message*, 2000
"The Final Audit" *Our Twentieth Century's Greatest Poems*, 1982
"The Miracle Heart" *Ideals Magazine*, 1995; *Beatrice (Neb) Daily Sun*, 2000
"Then He Reminds Me" *Nature's Echoes*, 2000; *www.poetry.com*, 2000
"Under the Wire" *Teachers of Vision*, 2013
"What Christmas Is" *Peoria Poetry Club Christmas*, 2002
"Wise men still seek the 'Star' of Bethlehem." *Touchstones of the Soul*, 1994
"Yesterday, Today, and Forever" *Peoria Poetry Club Christmas*, 1982

LIGHT FOR THE BURNING SOUL

Sparks, Flames, and Embers

CONTENTS

Dedication – iii
Acknowledgements - iv

A Note from the Author - 1

One	FINDING THE LIGHT - 3
Two	WALKING IN THE LIGHT - 33
Three	GRASPING FOR THE LIGHT - 49
Four	FOLLOWING THE LIGHT - 69
Five	SEARCHING FOR THE LIGHT - 81
Six	SHARING THE LIGHT - 99
Seven	AWED BY THE LIGHT - 115
Eight	BASKING IN THE LIGHT - 127

A Note from the Author

Few things in life are as rewarding, yet humbling, as being inspired by God to write about Him and for Him. The verses and anecdotes in *Light for the Burning Soul: Sparks, Flames, and Embers* are but a small measure of how He has blessed my personal walk with Him.

However you choose to read this book, my hope is that its pages will offer *sparks* of encouragement for those about to take their first steps with God; *flames* of excitement and joy for those already experiencing the walk; and *embers* of reassurance for all – lingering reminders that God is in control; that He always has been; and that He always will be.

One

FINDING THE LIGHT

*Son*shine puts the rainbow in my soul.

Listen ...

The Spirit of God
speaks in a whisper
and is heard only by those
who listen with their hearts.

There's a Name

There's a name I like to whisper;
There's a name I like to shout;
There's a name that I'm not willing
To go anywhere without.
There's a name that's always with me,
In my every thought and prayer:
It's the precious name of Jesus
That I carry everywhere.

I can shout it from the rooftop;
I can sing it soft and low;
For whatever way I say it,
He will answer me, I know.
For He's always there to listen,
Each and every day the same,
And I know He'll always hear me
When I speak His precious name.

There's a name that means tomorrow
Will be better than today,
For it wipes away my sorrow
And keeps all my fears at bay.
It's a name above all others
That I praise and set apart,
And I hold it ever near me,
On my lips and in my heart.

Jesus Is My Way of Life

I want to tell the story of my Savior's love
And how His dying set me free;
I want to sing and shout that He's alive again
And that He's coming back for me!
Alleluia! Jesus conquered sin and strife.
Alleluia! Jesus makes me high on Life.

I want to feast forever on the Living Bread
That Jesus offers me, and then
I want to quench my burning soul with Living Water
So I'll need not thirst again.
Alleluia! Jesus conquered sin and strife.
Alleluia! Jesus is my Way of Life.

I want to live in Heaven where there is no night
And where the streets are paved with gold;
Where I can walk with Jesus in a different Light
And where I never will grow old.
Alleluia! Jesus conquered sin and strife.
Alleluia! Jesus is my Friend for Life.

I want to share the Spirit of the glad new day
That Jesus' promises are of;
I want to sing His praises with the holy angels
In the presence of God's love.
Alleluia! Jesus conquered sin and strife.
Alleluia! Jesus is my Way of Life.

You Are the One

You are the One Who bids me lay
My burdens at Your feet each day.
You tell me all I need to do
Is raise my eyes and turn to You.

You are my Rock; You are my Everything;
You give me hope for Life; You are the Song I sing;
You are the Friend Who always stands by me;
You are the One Who set me free.

You are my Hope when things look grim;
You are my Light when others dim;
You never change; You are the same
No matter when I call Your name.

You are my Rock, the One I turn to first;
You are the Living Water that can quench my thirst;
You are my Strength when things go right or wrong;
You are the Spirit in my song.

You are the One Who holds my hand.
You lift me up and help me stand.
You never turn and walk away;
You are the Listener when I pray.

You are my Rock; You are the spoken Word;
You are the Bread of Life, my Brother, Savior, Lord.
You are the Evening Star that lights my way;
You are the Son that shines by day.

Gift of God

Out of pure love for a fallen world,
God supplied a heavenly plan –
precious gift of a Lifetime,
purchased with the scarlet
blood of the Lamb and
wrought with true love
through His Son's
nail-pierced
hands.

Prophet, Priest and King

My Lord came down, as man, to dwell
With hopeful sinners and dispel
The myth that they could not be loved by One like He;
The world could little understand
Why he would offer heart and hand
And let His precious blood be spilled for such as me.

My Lord was tempted as I am,
Became the sacrificial Lamb,
And with His life He paid the price I should have paid;
Though He was mocked and crucified,
He loved me even as He died,
But few could realize the sacrifice He made.

My Lord was placed inside a tomb
Amid Death's darkest hours of gloom,
But on the third day He arose to live again;
Then He ascended to prepare
A mansion far beyond compare,
And He'll return one day and take me with Him then.

The hour is close, so close at hand
When I'll be forced to take a stand,
But I'll be ready, as my Savior's hand I hold;
He's King of Kings and Lord of Lords!
His endless love for me affords
A Son-filled mansion in a city paved with gold.

My Lord is Prophet, Priest and King!
Past, present, future, everything
Depended solely on the love He had to give;
He is the Savior of my soul;
He offers Heaven as my goal;
He bore the burden of the cross that I might live.

Lift Your Voice and Rejoice!

There are too many things
To be happy about to be sad.
There are so many blessings
And Heavenly gifts to be had.
Jesus gives us a wonderful
Reason for living; I'm glad
There are too many things
To be happy about to be sad.

Put a smile on your face!
Jesus loves you, He wants you to know
He's always beside you,
To guide you, wherever you go;
Claim His promises,
Open your heart and let His light show:
Put a smile on your face!
Jesus loves you, He wants you to know.

Lift your voice and rejoice!
Don't you know you're a child of the King?
An heir of the Kingdom,
So shout it and let your heart sing!
Leave your burdens with Jesus,
He'll shelter you under His wing.
Lift your voice and rejoice!
Don't you know you're a child of the King?

There are too many things
To be happy about to be sad.
There are so many blessings
And Heavenly gifts to be had.
Jesus gives us a wonderful
Reason for living; I'm glad
There are too many things
To be happy about to be sad.

I Expect a Miracle Today

I expect a miracle today.
I won't let doubt or fear get in my way.
My heart will not be still;
I'll stand in faith until
My eyes have seen a miracle today.

I cannot know the love God has in store
Until I open up my heart for more.
I know He'll see me through
In all I say and do,
And I expect a miracle today.

God's love remains the same from day to day,
And miracles are just a prayer away.
I only need to speak
The comfort that I seek
And God will send a miracle my way.

Holding On to Jesus' Hand

When Satan struggles to deceive
And twist the truths that I believe,
I turn to Jesus, for I know
His nail-pierced hands won't let me go.
All earthly threats I can withstand
While holding on to Jesus' hand.

Though every avenue of life
Is filled with toil and sin and strife,
With patient fervor I will wait
To enter in at Heaven's gate.
The wide expanse will soon be spanned;
I'm holding on to Jesus' hand.

When death surrounds me and, at last,
Temptations of this life are past;
When I have entered into rest;
When Christ returns to claim the blessed,
I'll step into the Promised Land
Still holding on to Jesus' hand.

The Rising of the Son

When time began, a Father planned
A perfect world for man.
But jealousy and greed crept in
And changed the Father's plan.
And angels watched in glorious awe
The Father's sacrifice:
His only Son would have to pay
Redemption's purchase price.

Before things were, the Son had graced
His Father's side, and yet
He left His place in Heaven
To assume the sinner's debt.
The Son was nailed upon a cross,
And dark clouds billowed in
To separate the Father from
The horrors of the sin.

And the Father's heart was broken
For the deed that had been done,
But He looked beyond the darkness
To the rising of the Son.

Friends took the Son down from the cross
And placed Him in a tomb,
And soldiers stood outside to guard
The stone that sealed the room.

*And believers' hearts were shaken
For the deed that had been done,
But they held Isaiah's promise
Of the rising of the Son.*

Two days the Son lie, seemingly
Defeated by His foes,
But on the morning of the third,
The Father's Son arose!

*And Heaven rang with glory,
For the victory had been won
By the mercy of the Father
And the rising of the Son.*

Keep the Light On for Me, Lord

I've traveled far and near, Lord,
And Your signs are strong and clear
That this world is on a downward swing;
The end is drawing near.
The signal's flashing *CAUTION*
And Your warnings I behold:
Pay no mind to useless detours
That lead down the worldly road.

Keep the Light on for me, Lord, I'm comin' Home
To a mansion where I'll wish no more to roam.
By Your side, I know I'll never walk alone.
Keep the Light on for me, Lord, I'm comin' Home!

I'll soon be on my way to where
The skies are never gray;
Bread of Life and Living Water
To sustain me on my way.
There'll be others coming, too, Lord,
For they know the time is near;
Let Your Light shine ever brighter
So the pathway will be clear.

Keep the Light on for me, Lord, I'm comin' Home
To a mansion where I'll wish no more to roam.
By Your side, I know I'll never walk alone;
Keep the Light on for me, Lord, I'm comin' Home!

I Cannot Do It, but God Can

I cannot do it, but God can;
All things work better in His hands.
Whatever my burden, whatever my plight,
With God in the picture, my future looks bright.

So I put my worries in God's hands,
Seeing that His are the best plans;
And knowing, with things I just don't understand,
That I cannot do it, but God can.

The Hallelujah Railway Line

The Hallelujah Railway Line
Has a train that's Glory-bound,
But its whereabouts, to the unbelieving world
Cannot be found.
For its tracks were laid by One Who knew
That the railway line would fail
If a world of disbelief could cause
The Glory Train to be derailed.

While the train's still in the depot,
The Conductor does His share
To make sure that every well-deserving
Child of God is there.
As He passes through the cars and checks
With the passengers on board,
Every ticket reads *Paid In Advance
By Jesus Christ My Lord.*

Now the train will soon be ready
For that grand and glorious day
When she'll make her scheduled run
Without one stop along the way.
So her boiler's being fired up
With a Right-to-Glory goal,
And her whistle's being sounded out
To every living soul.

Ol' Satan's crouched along the track
Of the Hallelujah Line,
For he wants to keep that train from reaching
Glory-Land on time.

With his ear pressed tightly to the rail
And his feet on pleasure-ground,
He'll be listenin' for that Glory Train
'Cause he's gonna try to flag it down.

While he lies in wait, Satan meditates,
Then he plans his gruesome snare,
And he hopes to find, all along the line,
Open rails in disrepair.
To the track that's straight and narrow,
He will add sharp curves and bends,
And he'll try to switch that train to tracks
That lead to deadly ends.

But ... the engine's being readied
With a mighty head of steam,
And the Engineer is well aware
Of Satan's every scheme.
With His hand upon the throttle
And a mission that's divine,
He can take that train to Glory-Land
On the Hallelujah Railway Line.

If you're Heaven-bound and restless,
Climb aboard the Glory Train,
For its passengers have ought to lose
And everything to gain.
With her mighty whistle blowin'
She will get you Home on time,
So don't miss the run of the Glory Train
On the Hallelujah Railway Line.

I Have a Friend

I have a friend Who stands by me;
I have a Savior I long to see;
I have a loving Lord Who set me free;
I have a King Who reigns eternally.

My Friend is Jesus, God's only Son;
He is my Savior, Lord and King, all in One;
To save my wretched life from sin, He died alone,
But He'll come back one day to claim me as His own.

His Own Son's Hands

Only a loving Father
could fathom the depth of pure love
coming from the blood
of His own Son's hands
and make such a sacrifice
for one and all.

Scribbled in the Margin

The Book of Life will hold the names
Of those who've lived for You;
A full account of those who
Have been loyal, fast, and true.
And, Lord, I pray, as names
Are written there, row after row,
That there will be no question
As to where my name should go.

Whatever Your decision, Lord,
I will abide with it –
Just scribbled in the margin or
Wherever it will fit.
I don't care where it's written, Lord,
No special favors due;
I only need assurance
Of eternal Life with You.

The Maestro's Symphony

When God looked out over the wide expanse
of nothingness that would become Earth,
He saw that it needed music.

So He created mountains and hills
that break forth in song;
seas that roar;
thunder that has a voice;
floods that clap their hands;
trees that rejoice;
valleys that sing and shout for joy;
and a moon that is
faithful witness
to it all.

The earth trembles
and shakes
at His glory
as the Maestro conducts
His mighty symphony.

It's Up to You, Lord

It's up to You, Lord,
What would You have me do?
I trust your promises and know
You'll see me through.
You know my every thought;
You hear my every plea;
You know what's in my heart;
You know what's best for me.

It's up to You, Lord;
You are the knowing One;
Help me to always pray,
"Thy will be done."

Everything I Need

My Lord is Everything I need;
When I follow, He will lead.
Son of God and Son of man,
He has a never-changing plan.

Creator, Teacher, Healer, Friend,
His is a love that will not end.

Forecast of a *Life*time

Meteorologist turned pastor
gives Spirit-filled long-range forecast:
Son worshippers will dwell in
Sonshine and pleasant temps
as those who prefer
no Son at all
encounter
extreme
heat.

When Jesus Comes to Take Me Home

When Jesus comes in all His glory
To claim His loved ones as His own,
He'll complete the greatest Bible story
That this world of sin has ever known.
I'll meet Moses, Noah, and Elijah
At the River flowing from God's Throne;
And I'll walk beside my Lord forever
When Jesus comes to take me Home.

I'll see those I loved who've gone before me;
I'll see those I've never known before;
But the pain, the sorrow, and the suffering,
And the clouds of sin I'll see no more.
I'll hear all my favorite Bible stories
From the ones God chose to make them so;
And I'll walk beside my Lord forever
When Jesus comes to take me home.

I'll see flowers that will never wither,
But I'll never see the dark of night.
I'll see Jesus in His greatest splendor,
And I'll dwell forever in His Light.
I'll hear angels singing loud their praises,
And I'll walk the street that's paved with gold;
For I'll walk beside my Lord forever
When Jesus comes to take me Home.

Two

WALKING IN THE LIGHT

Because of God's love,
the Son takes on a different Light.

If Jesus Comes Tomorrow

If Jesus comes tomorrow,
Then I still have time today
To do the things that I've been
Putting off along the way;
I still have time to tell my friends
About His love for me
And how He died upon the cross
To set all sinners free.

Though ... if He comes tomorrow,
I have little time to waste
In reaching out to strangers
I've neglected in my haste.
But, then, I'm sure I'll find the time
To spread His precious Word
And pray that He will give me strength
To make His message heard.

I'm certain I can do it
If tomorrow's years away,
But will I be so confident
If Jesus comes ... *today*?

Whose Side Are You On?

Many lifetimes ago,
Jesus promised that He
Would come back with His angels
For you and for me.
Even now comes the voice
From the Spirit on high,
Asking who's on the Lord's side
As His coming draws nigh.

When Moses returned
With the tablets of stone,
His people had molded
A god of their own.
Through the camp, Moses gave
The resounding decree:
"Who's on the Lord's side?
Let him come unto me."

As Judas stood witness
To Jesus' 'defeat',
The kiss of betrayal
Turned bitterly sweet;
Though he pleaded, his offer
Could not be withdrawn.
On his heart lay the question,
"Whose side are you on?"

When his Lord needed friends,
Simon Peter denied
His acquaintance with the One
Who had stood by his side.
But he wept bitter tears
In the twilight of dawn
When his Savior's eyes questioned,
"Whose side are you on?"

Once the trumpets have sounded
Our Savior's return,
There'll be no time for voicing
Last-minute concern.
But for those who would listen,
He's making the plea:
"Who's on the Lord's side?
Let him come unto me."

The Savior is coming
For you and for me,
In the glory of Heaven,
That all eyes might see:
Will you hide in the shadows?
Will you stumble, or run?
Or are you ready to greet Him?
Whose side are you on?

Have You Met My Friend Named Jesus?

Have you met my Friend named Jesus,
Whose love is fast and strong?
Have you sought the peace He offers you
Amidst the busy throng?
Have you ever stopped to find Him
When things are going wrong
Or heard the notes of hope He sends
In every bluebird's song?

Did you meet with Him this morning
When the grass was wet with dew?
Or maybe just at twilight, when
Your weary day was through?
Did you see Him in the meadow,
In the sunset's amber hue?
If you met with Him at all today,
Then you know He's your Friend, too.

Taking the First Step

I stood in the shadows of worry and doubt,
Afraid to step forward, afraid to reach out.
Then, just like a beacon, His promise broke through:
"If you'll take the first step, I'll take the next two."

I wearied from struggling with goal after goal;
Misguided decisions had burdened my soul;
And not till I took Jesus' hand was I freed,
For He is the Answer to my every need.

The road's not been easy, and often I tell
Of times when I stumbled, of times when I fell;
But I have a Friend Who is also my Guide,
And when I'm in trouble, He's right by my side.

Tolerance Supreme

I'm all for zero tolerance
For drugs in sports and schools,
And "Three Strikes and You're Out" suits me
Just fine for other rules.
In fact, if I could have my way,
I would most likely say
Most punishments are far too lean
For those who disobey.
I've little time for child abusers,
Murderers, and such,
So sometimes I feel guilty 'cause
I just can't love them much.
Some things are easy to forgive,
But not so to forget.
My tolerance for foolery
Lies short of great, and yet …
I often think of God and
My relationship with Him
And wonder how He puts up with
My daily, willful sin.
I wonder how He watches
When I falter day by day
And still has love and patience
To wash all my sins away.

Knowing that it took
His own Son's blood to set me free,
I wonder how God finds the will
To love the likes of me.
I'm thankful for His mercy
When it comes to me and sin,
Lest, when it comes to Heaven's gates,
I fear I'd not get in.

Tomorrow

Tomorrow, I'll paint the pictures
That are in my mind today;
I hope I won't forget the scenes
I want so to portray.

Tomorrow, I'll take the time to stop
And see a friend or two,
Or do some things that others
Have been asking me to do.

Tomorrow, I'll find the time to sit
And reminisce awhile;
Take time to see a sunset
Or to catch a baby's smile.

Tomorrow, I'll linger on the path
And smell the roses there,
But I can't stop today,
For I have little time to spare.

I may have time tomorrow,
But I have no time today,
For busy schedules that I've made
Keep getting in the way.

Not long ago, I met a man
With plans as big as I;
I wonder – did he get them done?
Or did he up and die?

God's "Wanted" List

When God declares the end of time,
When Jesus gazes down the line,
Will I be on His *Wanted* list?
Or will my name be one that missed?

The Choice is Mine

When life is threatened by the hopelessness of sin,
I know there's One who waits outside to be let in.
Though I may try my best to do things on my own,
When things get rough, I know I need not walk alone.

When pathways crumble and I stumble, or I fall,
I know there's One who walks beside me through it all.
I only need to take the first step on my own.
The choice is mine; I know I need not walk alone.

When problems overcome and leave my mind perplexed,
I take the first step and He helps me take the next.
He'll never leave and let me struggle on my own.
When all is said and done, I need not walk alone.

Never Tiring

I never get tired of sunsets;
I seldom get upset with rain;
I never get tired of dewdrops
Or frost on a window pane.

I welcome each beautiful sunrise
And birds that come daily to feed;
I never get tired of knowing
That God fills my every need.

I never get tired of praying,
No matter the time or the place;
I never get tired of knowing
That one day I'll look on His face.

When God Steps In

It seems, when good things happen,
People always pass the buck.
They blame the bad on God, yet chalk
The good things up to "luck."
Oft' times, the hand of Fate has put
My courage on the run
And made me well aware I've been
Protected by Someone.
So when I hear the words *What luck!*
I treat them with chagrin,
For I know it isn't luck at all,
That God has just stepped in.

Priceless Treasure

'Priceless' treasures haunt men's souls;
With gold, they seek to bind:
No matter what the cost, they'll buy
The treasures that they find.
In vain they search and waste their time;
In vain, for can't they see?
The only priceless treasure
Has been paid for, and it's free.

The price was paid by One who gave
His all that we might live;
The treasure is the gift of Life –
What more can one Man give?

Three

GRASPING FOR THE LIGHT

It isn't *what* you know, but *Who* you know,
that'll get you where you want to go.

A Special Invitation

I have a Friend who's written me
The most exciting letter!
It's filled with stories just so I
Can get to know Him better.

In story after story,
There's a standing invitation,
To meet with Him and join Him
In a special celebration.

His Heavenly host will all be there,
And friends I long to see,
So every day, My Lord receives
My R.S.V.P.

Make Me Worthy

The Court lies in readiness;
Heralds are poised at its gates.
The Kingdom is being made ready
While all Heaven waits.
With glad alleluias,
Ten thousands of angels will sing.
Please, Lord, make me worthy
To enter the Court of the King.

The King, in His splendor,
Will soon be approaching the Throne
To claim what He painfully purchased
With His blood alone.
Like Esther, I've nothing,
Except for the faith that I bring,
So, Lord, make me worthy
To enter the Court of the King.

The jester is anxious
To answer His last curtain calls,
Though he'll be the fool
Who'll be fooled when the last curtain falls.
In vain, he's deceived
And disguised every guise of death's sting;
His farewell performance
Can only be topped by the King.

The trumpets are lifted!
Their glorious sound will soon break
The silence of death
As the heirs of the Kingdom awake
To enter the Court
As the bells of Eternity ring!
Please, Lord, make me worthy
To enter the Court of the King.

The Miracle Heart

The label read *Fragile. Handle with love.*
Contents: One Miracle Heart from above.
If personalization of heart is desired,
Just follow these steps. (Some assembly required.)

Step One said *Take your love plus My love for you*
And fill up the heart, then proceed to Step Two.
So I gathered some love that I knew was from Him
And, with most of my love, filled the heart to the brim,
Holding back just a little in case of a spill,
Being careful to keep the heart quiet and still.

Step Two said *If love doesn't flow from the heart,*
Then the heart did not open; go back to the start;
And just to make certain Step One is complete:
When the love starts to flow, then you'll hear the heart beat.
But if, after all, love still fails to flow,
Then check, step by step, 'Troubleshooting' below.

Well, of course, I knew better. I chiseled and tried
To pry open the heart with the love locked inside;
But love just wasn't flowing, with all that I'd done,
So I stubbornly turned back to Step Number One.
Over and over I read it again,
But before I gave up, I finally gave in.
When I checked 'Troubleshooting' to see what was wrong,
I found the instructions were right all along.

For it read *You must follow Step One to a 'T',*
*Using **all** of your love, plus that given by Me.*
So don't hold any back, and if any should spill,
Let it flow out to others who still need their fill.
Just make sure that you follow this step every day,
For your love cannot grow till you give it away;
But the heart isn't yours till the love in it grows,
And no miracle comes till the heart overflows.

So I re-filled the heart till its love overflowed,
Till it beat with a rhythm that couldn't be slowed,
And then, in the fine print, read *Let it be known*
That this Miracle Heart is now truly your own.

The Final Audit

The Balance Sheet was finished,
The Ledger finalized,
The records of a lifetime
To be closely scrutinized.
The Auditor stood ready
To examine every line
In order to determine
The fate that would be mine.

As He surveyed the Balance Sheet,
My heart was filled with dread,
For all my assets could not match
The entries made in red.
The liabilities of sin
Had plagued my life since birth.
The simple words *I love my Lord*
Summed up my total worth.

He opened up the Ledger,
And I held my breath in fear,
For knowing eyes could see beyond
Notations entered here.
The only credits posted were
Faith, Hope, and *Charity;*
The entry under 'Debits' read
My Savior died for me.

The books could not be balanced,
I acknowledged with regret,
For all the records showed
That I was deeply in His debt.
Then nail-scarred hands re-marked the books
And handed them to me,
And when I checked them once again,
They balanced perfectly.

The assets on my Balance Sheet
Read *Riches yet untold,*
And there, in bold, red letters
Was the *Loss of Satan's hold.*
The credits in my Ledger
Were summed up *Redeemable,*
While written under 'Debits'
Was a simple *Paid in full.*

The Buyer's Fingerprints

Inside a dimly-lighted shop,
A potter knelt to pray.
He said, "Dear Lord, please bless me
As I come to You today,
For I am like a vessel
That cannot be sold or bought:
I'm broken, weak, and shattered,
And my value comes to naught."

No sooner had he said Amen
Than a Buyer came that way
And asked to see the potter's wares—
All vessels made of clay.
The Buyer, walking down each aisle,
Paused briefly at each shelf;
Picked each and every vessel up
And hugged it to Himself.

The anxious potter studied
Every move the Buyer made
And wondered at the Buyer's
Unique interest in his trade.
He thought to lead the Buyer
To his better jars, but no,
The Buyer stayed among the ones
He usually would not show.

The potter softly questioned,
"Sir, what are You looking for?"
The Buyer said, "I came to buy
The broken ones, and more."

The potter hurried to retrieve
Each less-than-perfect jar —
Discarded ones with cracks and flaws;
Not one without a scar.

He didn't doubt the Buyer's words,
Yet wondered why He'd care
To buy such useless vessels
That seemed far beyond repair;
But, just the same, he set them up
Amidst the jars he prized
And left them to the Buyer,
To be better scrutinized;

And when the shop was filled with Light,
The potter stood in awe:
But for the Buyer's fingerprints,
Not one jar had a flaw.
The Buyer's hands, clay-covered now,
Showed scars that nails had made,
And every jar on every shelf
Was labeled BOUGHT and PAID.

The Buyer left; the potter knelt
And said, "I thank You, God,
For showing me I'm savable,
However weak or flawed.
Reshape me as a vessel
Of your love, that all may see
Distinct impressions
Of the Buyer's fingerprints on me."

The Beacon in the Lighthouse

The flag inside the Harbor warned
Of rough and stormy seas
But, sailor that I was, I spurned
The Harbormaster's pleas;
Yet in His eyes reflected,
With the gentle love He bore,
The semblance of the Beacon
In the Lighthouse on the shore.

The course I chose to follow
Boasted Freedom to be gained,
But in the vastness of the sea
My Spirit fairly waned;
And not until I'd lost sight
Of the Beacon did I learn
That somewhere just past Freedom
Lay the Point of No Return.
I had no time to linger,
For the storm was closing in
And, if I would be safe,
I must go back to where I'd been.
I prayed that it was not too late,
But when I turned around
I saw ships battered hopelessly,
And some had run aground.

My only hope for Life was that
I keep a lookout for
The never-failing Beacon
In the Lighthouse on the shore.
Then, overcoming darkness
Such as only Death can claim,
The Beacon Light pierced through the night
With ever-perfect aim.

Through tears and blinding rain,
I fixed my eyes upon that Light
And focused all my being
On just keeping it in sight.
The way was rough and rocky,
And the storm did not subside
Until I'd reached the Harbor
And was safely moored inside.

The Harbormaster fostered
No contempt for what I'd done.
Instead, He showed forgiveness
As a Father to His son,
While in His eyes reflected,
With the gentle love He bore,
The semblance of the Beacon
In the Lighthouse on the shore.

The Potter's Hands

The Potter's hands were steady
As He formed the man of clay
And breathed into his nostrils
The breath of life that day:
A vessel in His likeness,
Without a single flaw.
The man became a living soul
As angels watched in awe.

He filled the vessel to the brim
With love, to overflow
Into more vessels He would make
To assure the love would grow.
But, all too soon, the vessels cracked;
Love seeped out and was lost,
And the Potter's hands were forced to mend
The cracks at His own cost.

Now the Potter's hands have nail scars
That will never disappear,
For each crack in every vessel
Needs His constant, daily care.
And although they are not perfect yet,
Each vessel can lay claim
To the promise it will be made new
In the Potter's holy name.

Excess Baggage

The plane was on the runway
When the message was relayed
That, due to straggling passengers,
The flight would be delayed.
I hurried through the crowd,
But as I reached the boarding gate,
The captain stepped in front of me
And said, "You'll have to wait."

"But, Sir!" I said, "You do not seem
To understand my plight:
I fear that if I don't get through,
I'll surely miss my flight!
You see, it is by special invitation
That I go
To see my Savior, Lord, and King
Because He loves me so."

The Captain smiled and said,
"The invitation you received
Was given by My Father
On the day you first believed.
And though you're scheduled for this flight,
Somehow you have ignored
The fact that no one's excess baggage
Can be brought aboard."

Again, I said, "But, Sir!
I carry nothing! I'm afraid
I've nothing here that must be checked
And nothing to be weighed.
I come with only love,
My only destination, Life,
My priceless fare prepaid by One
Who conquered sin and strife."

The Captain didn't waver
But said lovingly to me,
"Although your hands are empty,
It's a troubled soul I see;
For, in your haste to please the world,
You've failed to set apart
The burdens of a lifetime
That weigh heavy on your heart.

"At one time, you surrendered everything
For Heaven's sake,
But then you chose to bear alone
Your guilt for each mistake.
Too long you've carried loneliness
Held fast by senseless pride
And covered well with anger
That you've done your best to hide."

I had no ready answer,
For the Captain's words were true.
He said, "How oft' would I have carried
Everything for you.
Yet now, if you would board this flight
And take your rightful seat,
You only need to place
Your excess baggage at My feet."

Right then and there I opened up
My heart and soul to bare
A world of useless feelings
That I'd always known were there.
I looked into the Captain's eyes,
Then dropped on bended knee
And cried, "Lift all these burdens from me, Lord,
And set me free."

Now the plane's still on the runway,
Pending clearance from Above;
The Captain is receiving all
Who won't deny His love.
But if you hope to catch this flight
And claim your rightful seat,
Take time right now to place
Your excess baggage at His feet.

Four

FOLLOWING THE LIGHT

The Light of God floods every corner of the heart
while crowding out only the darkness.

After the Storm

There is a rainbow
after every storm;
whether or not you see it
depends on how much Light
is in your soul.

The Light from Heaven's Window

I was lingering in the shadows
Of a dimly-lit street
When the ground that I was walking on
Gave way beneath my feet.
The sky gave way to emptiness
Devoid of sun or moon;
I longed to get to higher ground
But knew it must be soon.

In the throes of desperation,
I groped to find my way,
Still sinking in the hollow gloom
That all around me lay.
"Dear Lord," I cried, "don't let me fall!
Please let Your Light shine here!"
'Twas then the faintest whisper deftly
Fell upon my ear:

"My child, I'm here to help you,
For I've heard your fervent call;
I'm here to walk beside you,
And I will not let you fall;
But yet there is one step of faith
That you must take alone:
Step over to the other path;
It's made of Rock and stone.
Although it's straight and narrow,
It will never let you down;
It has a strong Foundation
For those seeking higher ground."

My Spirit soared with freedom
As my deepest fears took flight,
For deep within my soul I knew
The narrow way was right;
And when I set my foot out toward
The path I could not see,
The Light from Heaven's window fell
Upon the Rock, for me;
And once again the promise
That fell deftly over all:
"I'm here to walk beside you,
And I *will not* let you fall."

S.O S. to Heaven!

S.O.S. to Heaven!
I got lost on my way Home!
I took a well-worn detour;
Now I'm struggling all alone
To find the straight and narrow path
That leads to Heaven's Gate,
For if I don't get back there soon,
It might just be too late.

I was heading Homeward
When a stranger said to me,
"The detour is a wider road
With so much more to see."
I followed his suggestion,
But his path led me astray.
S.O.S. to Heaven!
Please send Someone right away!

Out here, there's a world of lights
To lure me from my goal,
But not a one can lighten up
The darkness in my soul.
I need the Son to light my path,
A Guide to lead me Home;
S.O.S. to Heaven!
I can't get there on my own!

I feel the darkness lifting,
Artificial lights grown dim;
I hear my Savior calling me
To turn and follow Him...

S.O.S. to Heaven!
Through my tears, I see the Light!
The signs are pointing Homeward,
And I have the Road in sight!
I only have to take my Savior's hand,
Without delay.
S.O.S. to Heaven:
Lead me Homeward day by day.

The Path

I'd seen the path He'd pointed out
As I'd hurried on my way,
But, in my haste, I'd passed it by
To take another day.
I feared I could not find it now,
Though in my heart I knew
That He would lead me back to it
If I'd just ask Him to.

But guilt weighed heavy on my heart,
For He'd been good to me,
Though I had followed darker paths
Against His every plea.
They'd led me in directions
That I knew I shouldn't go;
They'd put my Life in jeopardy
And kept my spirits low.

And when things started going wrong,
I shuddered, for I knew
I'd had a chance to go His way
Each time He'd asked me to.
This time, I'd seek His help,
Unlike the many times before
When I had turned my back on Him
As He'd stood at my door.

I whispered, "Lord, I know You're there;
Please let me see a sign.
I want to go with You, if You'll
Invite me one more time.
I want the path that leads to Life
And steers away from sin.
I've opened up the door now, Lord,
And pray that You'll come in."

I turned to see a gentle Soul
With eyes and smile aglow,
Who said, "I know the path you seek.
Together, let us go."
Without a second thought this time,
I've let Him lead the Way,
Content in knowing He is here
To help me day by day.

Open the Door

The heart is the door to the soul.
Close it, and the soul
withers and dies in darkness.
Open it to Light and Living Water,
and the soul becomes
a flourishing garden
tended by God's own hand.

Five

SEARCHING FOR THE LIGHT

Tears shape the rainbow of the soul.

Let Go of the Oars

I was on my way home
When the darkening sky
Showed the "storm in the distance"
Drawn terribly nigh.
Alone on the sea,
I rowed all through the night,
Though I saw no relief
And no shelter in sight.

With small hope of survival,
I whispered a prayer
And cried, in my blindness,
"Lord, don't You care?"
But just when I thought
It was useless to pray,
A hand touched my shoulder,
And I heard Someone say,

"Let go of the oars.
Stop trying to row,
For the course you've been taking
Is futile, you know.
Let Me sit here beside you;
I'll quiet the sea.
Take your hands off the oars ...
Leave the rowing to me."

A Prayer for You

I said a prayer for you today –
That God would bless you in some way;
For He alone knows thoughts and deeds,
And He alone supplies our needs.
So, whether skies are gray or blue,
Remember, God will see you through.

Answers Yet to Come

I can't begin to count my prayers,
The old ones or the new,
The favors and the pardons, God,
That I have asked of You;
Some prayers so long forgotten
And the ones that have become
Filed, to be repeated, under
Answers yet to come.

A Good "Heart" Cleaning

I knew it would come to this,
knew I'd misplace it sooner or later
in all this mess ...

someone asked me for it
just the other day,
but I couldn't find it ...

maybe if I open the doors,
let in some Light ... hmmm ...
never noticed those webs before
or those ugly rumors struggling to get free ...
better pull those down ...
push past these bad feelings and bits of gossip
floating here and there and everywhere ...
should get rid of them all
but ... maybe if I just
shove them to the back ...
there's room right back there in the corner ...
oops! that's God's *love* back there ...

better move *that* up front
and keep looking ... *ah!* there it is ...
my willingness to forgive ...

better keep it handy,
just in case someone
asks me for it again.

The Fork in the Road

As you travel Life's Highway,
Take heed what you choose
When you come to the fork in the road,
Where the highway divides
And each traveler decides
On the wide or the narrower road.

The narrow's not easy,
For detours abound
And, although you'll be tempted to stray,
Where Life is at stake,
You'll know which road to take
If you'll pause for a moment, to pray.

For there's One Who is waiting
To see what you'll do
When you come to the fork in the road.
If you choose Him as Guide,
He will walk by your side,
And He'll willingly carry your load.

When the weight of decision
Is getting you down;
When each sign that you see reads *This Way;*
Will you stand there in doubt?
Take the easy way out?
Or will you take a moment to pray?

Lord, Don't You Hear?

On the brink of desperation,
With so many things to do,
I knew the plans I'd made were not
Enough to see me through.
I said, "Lord, help me do it all;
You see, I have these plans;
But, Lord, they just aren't working,
And I need some helping hands."

It seemed He wasn't listening,
So I called, "Lord, don't You hear?
I've so much to accomplish;
I'll not finish it, I fear!"
Then the sweetest of all whispers said,
"I know your every need;
Just put your hand in My hand,
And let Me take the lead."

I didn't need much coaxing, then,
But once He took my hand,
I realized that things would not
Be going as I'd planned:
The things I'd thought to work out first
Got bumped to very last,
And things I'd tried avoiding
Bounced ahead and got done fast.

Today, with joy, I seek His help
As, hour by hour, I learn:
His hand is there to steady mine
Whichever way I turn.
And if my grip begins to slip,
I willingly concede,
"Please take my hand in Your hand, Lord;
I'll follow where You lead."

Then He Reminds Me

When life seems hopeless from my narrow point of view;
When I question why things happen as they do;
When I feel I cannot face life on my own,
Then He reminds me that I never walk alone.

He sees me tempted, and He shows me right from wrong;
He sees me doubtful, and He fills my heart with song;
He sees me saddened by a temporary loss;
Then He reminds me that He died upon the cross.

He sees me falling, and He stoops to pick me up;
He sees me thirsting, and He stops to fill my cup;
He sees me troubled when I think that I can't win;
Then He reminds me that He came to conquer sin.

He sees me lost and volunteers to be my Guide;
He sees me lonely, and his arms open wide;
He sees me shackled by my guilt and misery;
Then He reminds me that His dying set me free.

He sees me weary, and He lightens up my load;
He sees me stumble, and He stops to clear the road;
He sees I'm sorry for the countless sins I bring;
Then He reminds me: He's my Savior, Lord and King.

The Knock at My Door

Alone and pressed for time, I heard
A knock upon my door
And opened it to find a Man
I'd seen somewhere before.
I did my best to shut him out,
Convinced I couldn't spare
A precious moment of my time
To hear about his wares.
But as he stood there,
Shadowed by the darkness of my sin,
I put my doubts behind me,
Stepped aside, and asked Him in.

He talked about a mansion
In a city paved with gold,
Where Light will shine forever
And nobody will grow old;
Where flowers will not wither
And no sickness will invade;
Where death will be forgotten
And where love will never fade.
Although it sounded like a place
I'd gladly go to live,
I said, "It must be costly, Sir,
I've not one cent to give."

He said, "You need not worry —
Earthly riches count for naught;
The privilege of living in *this* City
Can't be bought.
You see, I paid the price for all,
So every soul is free
To claim the gift of Life;
You only need to follow Me."

Then, as He turned to leave, He said,
"The choice is up to you,
But I'll not pass this way again
Unless you ask me to."

I could not let Him walk away
Not knowing where or when
I'd have the opportunity
To see His face again.

I said, "I'll go, but what if I
Get lost along the way?"
He said, "Just keep your eyes on Me;
I will not let you stray.
But if, by chance, you look away
And step in sinking sand,
Just look for Me; I'll be right there;
Reach out and take My hand."

I keep my eyes upon Him now
And follow where He leads;
I worry not about the past
Or of my future needs.
I follow in His footsteps,
Knowing He supplies my all;
That He's right there to pick me up
Each time I trip and fall.
No longer do I let doubt rule,
For more and more I see
A mansion in the City
Where He paid it all, for me.

Keep Your Eyes upon the Savior

Keep your eyes upon the Savior;
Turn your thoughts to Him today;
He's waiting and He's watching,
So don't turn and look away.
With hands outstretched and ready,
He will lift you from life's harms;
Keep your eyes upon the Savior
And find shelter in His arms.

Keep your eyes upon the Savior
As you hurry through your day;
If you keep Him always in your sight,
You'll find it hard to stray.
While other friends may help you find
What leads to worldly gain,
The Savior gives the gift of Life Eternal
Through His name.

With danger lurking everywhere
And strife on every side,
He promises to give you hope
And be your daily Guide.
He's waiting now with open arms
To see what you will do.
Keep your eyes upon the Savior,
For He'll never fail you.

Calling On God

I'm thankful to know, when my worries "convene,"
That God doesn't have a recording machine.
I'm thankful that there is no time, night or day,
When He'll be too busy and turn me away.

No chance of misdialing; I just speak His name.
There's only one God, and He's always the same.
His line's never busy; I'm not put on hold;
He has all the answers, for young and for old.

I don't have to sit through a musical score
Or choose from a menu of one, two, three, four.
I never feel hurried – no cut-offs, no cost,
And there's never a fear that my call will be lost.

I'm thankful, when kneeling, before a night's sleep,
That God doesn't tell me to wait for the beep.

Six

SHARING THE LIGHT

God touches our hearts through others' hands.

Faithful Witness

Nothing
can shake the faith
of a mother
who has witnessed
miracles.

Blessed by God

Mothers are so blessed by God
that He passes on His touch through their hands,
His hugs through their arms,
and His love through their hearts.

In the Hands of Angels

A heart is not a simple thing
That God just throws together,
For each new heart must be prepared
For storms that it must weather.

A heart must have some room for love
And lots of room for caring,
Along with room for peace and joy,
For faith, and hope, and sharing.

A heart must be equipped
With flexibility for bending,
And yet, if it should break,
It must be capable of mending.

It needs some curiosity
And just a pinch of knowing;
But, most of all, it needs a place
Where it can keep on growing.

So God prepares each heart with love
And, then, with perfect measure,
His heavenly angels place them
In the little ones we treasure.

Under the Wire

A teacher who had lost her knack
For keeping spirits high
Was on the verge of quitting
When a Gardener happened by.
The Gardener asked no questions
Of the teacher but, instead,
He pointed at a vine outside
The window as He said,

"To reach new heights, a vine needs
Motivation, and a goal;
But know that, as you nurture it
And train it as a whole,
The only way it can survive
Is if each branch is free
To share its beauty through
Its individuality.

"To teach is but to learn anew,
For teaching takes no prize
Unless it sheds new light on learning
Through another's eyes;
While, through the light of learning shines
The privilege to teach
That hopes and dreams and miracles
Lie well within one's reach."

The teacher listened thoughtfully
To words she knew were true
And kept a watchful eye on vine
And students as they grew.

But, as the days drew longer,
She was painfully aware
That spring had come and gone
And all the branches were still bare.

So, high above the tendrils,
She worked deftly to secure
A wire barely visible
To anyone but her;
Then, with a gardener's patience,
Watched the branches day by day,
Content to offer guidance only
When they went astray.

At last, small buds appeared,
Each one unfolding to expose
A grand uniqueness of its own –
Each one a precious rose.
And though each rose was different,
Each one had the same desire:
To be the best that it could be
While reaching for the wire.

Though some reached up and some reached out,
They all reached deep within
To find the strength and stamina
They knew they'd need to win.
And in the end, they realized
The prize they could assay
Was not the goal itself,
But what they'd learned along the way.

A Teacher's Prayer

Lord, let me find the words to reach
These little ones I've come to teach;
These little ones to whom belong
The gift of innocence and song.
Give extra patience when I'm pressed
And courage, Lord, to face each test.
Let every blessing I receive
Reflect on those who would believe,
That they might learn to lean on You
In all they say, in all they do.

Working with Angels

My sister and brother-in-law were miles from home when a tornado ripped off part of their roof, destroyed their garage, and twisted twenty full-grown trees out of the ground. In an attempt to lessen the blow and protect their exposed belongings, eighteen relatives and friends gathered to cut, carry, haul, and rake.

We were all happy for the added assistance of a man who seemed to appear out of nowhere, with his own wheelbarrow and rake. Asked if he was a friend of the owners, the man replied, "I don't even know them, but they certainly aren't enemies."

The mystery was solved when my sister arrived home, and we found that our mysterious helper was the pastor of the church up the road.

The Shirt off His Back

One blustery winter evening, our young assistant pastor stopped by for a short visit. He was distraught at a gaping hole in the back of his topcoat – the result of standing too close to an open heater in the home of an elderly lady.

My husband disappeared for a moment, returning with a camel-colored cashmere coat he had inherited from my stepfather. He held the coat for the pastor, who gratefully put it on while promising to return it as soon as he could replace his own. I was not surprised when my husband insisted that the coat was not a loan, but a gift.

A Twist of "Limon"

My husband and I were traveling through Colorado one winter night when a blizzard forced the closing of Interstate 80. State Troopers stood at barricades, guiding traffic to an off-ramp that funneled us directly into the little town of Limon. After a disheartening string of *NO VACANCYs,* we and many others were thankful for a Baptist Church whose gymnasium was equipped with mats, blankets, games and videos, plus an ample supply of soft drinks and fresh, hot pizza delivered on the spot, all free of charge.

When word came that the interstate had been partially cleared, we dropped a check in an inconspicuous donation box and got underway. A few weeks later, we received a thank you note with a receipt marked *"Limon-Aid."*

Angel in the Work Force

My young daughter-in-law was heading for work on the interstate early one morning when the engine of her car died. Letting the car coast to the shoulder, she prayed that someone would stop to help her. Someone did. Another woman, also on her way to work, offered the use of jumper cables, called a towing company, and insisted on staying right there until she knew that the car was running.

While they waited, my daughter-in-law expressed concern that the woman would be late for work and would surely get into trouble with her company. Her fears were put to rest with a friendly arm around her shoulder followed by, "Honey, don't worry about me. I *own* the company."

Praise the Lord

It was obvious by their dress and their speech that the two young men in the booth behind us were from the nearby group home for the slightly handicapped. But it wasn't their dress or their speech that caught my attention; rather, it was their conversation and the fact that they were emptying their pockets of change.

Placing all they had on the table, they painstakingly began to add: "A nickel," one said quietly. "That's five cents; and a quarter, that's twenty-five... thirty cents... " And on it went, nickel by nickel and quarter by quarter. Then the disappointing conclusion: not enough money between them for the movie theater.

I relayed their overheard disappointment to my husband, who immediately walked back to their table, pulled out his wallet, and handed them each enough money to get into the theater, suggesting they spend their change on something else.

Thanking us repeatedly, the young men asked our names and thanked us yet again. Then, as my husband came back and sat down, they whisper in unison, heads bowed, "Thank You, Lord ... thank You, Lord."

Seven

AWED BY THE LIGHT

Wise men still seek the 'Star' of Bethlehem.

Yesterday, Today, and Forever

City streets a bustle
With the sounds of evening trade;
Travelers seeking lodging;
Heavy taxes to be paid;
Spirit of the season,
And all Reason, pushed aside
By greed that knows no boundaries
In a world of human pride ...

Baby Jesus in a manger:
Holy, lowly place;
Animals that He created
Gazing on His face;
Angels whispering lullabies
That make all Heaven ring;
Satan seeking to destroy
The Baby through a king ...

Shepherds tending sleeping flocks
As angels come to them;
Wise men following the star
That leads to Bethlehem;
Heavenly Father looking on
With love that shaped the plan
Of sacrifice, in sending down
His only Son for man.

What Christmas Is

Christmas *isn't* packages
Wrapped up in fancy bows;
Christmas *isn't* Santa Claus
Or elves with turned-up toes;
Christmas *isn't* rushing out
To catch the latest sale,
Or finding time to drop
Last-minute greetings in the mail.

But Christmas *is* the love that snugs
The bows of family ties;
And Christmas *is* the hope that glows
In children's watchful eyes.
Christmas *is* the faith that comes
From knowing One could be
So filled with love that He'd agree
To give His life for me.

A Child Shall Lead Them

A well-known Teacher stood beside
The road of Life one day
And greeted every traveler who,
By choice, had walked that way.
Among the weak and weary ones
A mother stopped to rest
As tenderly she held her tiny
Infant to her breast.

The Teacher's heart grew heavy
For the mother's silent cries;
The mother dropped her head
So not to look into His eyes.
"Why do you tarry so?" He asked.
*"You promised long ago
That you would lead this infant
In the way that he should go."*

The mother said, *"It seems to me
An overwhelming task,"*
But as she sat there pondering
She felt compelled to ask,
*"How can I teach him 'trust' and 'faith'
And how can I succeed
In making sure this little one
Will follow where I lead?"*

The Teacher placed a tender hand
Upon the infant's head,
And as He took the infant
From the mother's arms, He said,
"A child can only learn to trust
Through love that he receives,
But from that trust comes faith to hope
For all that he believes.
The learning of a child is not
Unlike a bird that sings:
You cannot hope to share it
If you miss the joy it brings.
So if you'd lead a little one,
Don't hesitate to turn
And look behind you, for it's from
The little ones we learn.

"A child can only learn to speak
By proving what he's heard,
But in his eagerness to learn
He clings to every word.
He only learns to walk by letting go
Of what he's known
And yet, in stepping out, he knows
He need not walk alone.

*The need to share is witnessed
By the way the child lives,
For precious measures of himself
The child freely gives.
By taking his example
On the Road of Life, you'll find
The little one you hope to lead
Will follow right behind."*

The Teacher's gentle message
Calmed the mother's greatest fears
And, as He held her little one,
Her eyes welled up with tears.
She simply couldn't understand
Why One so great as He
Would want to hold a little child
Like hers upon His knee.

The Teacher, sensing every thought,
Reflected as He smiled,
*"I left My home in Heaven to
Become a little Child."*

One Life to Give

While shepherds watched their flocks by night,
An angel donned in Heaven's light
Brought joyful tidings, peace on earth,
News of the long-awaited birth.

In Bethlehem that very morn
The sacrificial Lamb was born.

The First Christmas Gift

No room in the inn, the innkeeper said,
But he offered a stable with hay, for a bed;
And a star settled over the stable that night,
And the King of all glory was born in its light;
And shepherds, rejoicing, left hillside and fold,
While wise men brought spices of incense and gold;
And angels sang praises from Heaven above,
All to honor the first Christmas Gift of God's love.

Eight

BASKING IN THE LIGHT

God smiles through the eyes of a child.

Turnabout

My sister's hands were full of knitting when her young son asked her to turn on the light in his room so that he could get his toys. Convincing him that he need only take God's hand and God would go with him, she watched him disappear into the hallway and saw the light come on. He returned a few minutes later, toys in hand. But when she reminded him that he'd forgotten to turn off the light, he replied, "It's all right, Mom. God'll turn it out."

Off the Tip of Her Tongue

Shortly after news from friends, of "Baby Noah's" birth, our young granddaughter rushed up to Noah's mother with a baby gift, announcing, "This is a present for Baby … um … um … *Moses!*"

No Doubt about It

During a Bible lesson about choices, each kindergartner was given an imaginary situation involving a friend or sibling and asked who should get first choice.

When it came to herself, a friend, and two different-sized cookies, one little girl's imaginary friend got first choice. Likewise, with computer games shared by brothers, a little boy said that his older brother would get to choose which game to play.

Then came the last youngster, to whom I said, "Pretend that you and your sister are getting into the car, and you both want to sit in the same seat. Who gets to choose where you will sit?"

Without hesitation, he said, "Our *parents!*"

Convincing the Invincible

After listening intently to the Bible story in which Jesus healed Peter's mother-in-law, our pastor's four-year-old daughter carried it a bit further by adding, "But she died later."

I assured her with, "Oh, yes. We *all* have to die sooner or later."

While most of the kids let the latter thought go right over their heads, one little boy looked directly into my eyes and said, "Well, *I'm* not going to die – sooner *or* later!"

In the Presence of Angels

Bible verses were a snap for our large kindergarten class. By the end of thirteen weeks, most of our four-to-seven-year olds could recite all thirteen verses without hesitation and were happy to speak loudly into my tape recorder. One recitation of Luke 15:10 ended up as: "There is rejoicing in the presidents of the angels of God over one sinner who repents."

Hey, Lord, Remember Me?

When given their choice of songs to sing, our kindergartners never failed to choose "Do Lord," and then proceeded to sing with all their might. But one little guy's voice always boomed out over the others, asking, "Do Lord, oh, do Lord, oh, do you remember me?"

Leading His Lambs

My husband was sporting his annual winter beard the day he led a leashed pet lamb into our church kindergarten room and let the children pet and feed it. Later, a father stopped by to say that his five-year-old son had run to him after class and excitedly said, "Daddy! We had a real live shepherd today!"

Hard to Swallow?

With our Bible lesson on sharing, I divided a large cinnamon roll into eight wedges. After choosing the wedge he wanted, one little boy immediately took an enormous bite. Concerned that he might choke, I warned all of the children to "chew it up really well," to which another replied, "Don't you want us to swallow it?"

Lending a Hand

At their Cradle Roll table, two three-year-old boys (one a Filipino American, the other an African American) were asked how many days come before God's day of rest. When both boys agreed on six, the first was asked to count them.

As he slowly opened the fingers and thumb of his right hand and spread them on the table, the teacher, who was also his mother, counted with him, "... three, four, five, ... " hesitating only when he did and finally asking, "But where is the sixth?" The puzzled look on the boy's face brought the other boy quietly to his feet. Without a word, he reached across the table and placed the index finger of his left hand next to his friend's thumb.

While Shepherds Watched

While telling the Christmas story, I asked our small class of kindergarteners what the shepherds were doing out on the hillside the night Baby Jesus was born. "Watching their *flops*," was the quick reply from one six-year-old.

Determined not to embarrass him, I said, very distinctly, "That's right. They were watching their *flocks*."

When a quick review of the story brought about the same question, the same little boy piped up with, "Watching their ... *sheep*."

Substitute "Owner"

After a short absence from church and teaching, I asked my kindergarten class who had taken my place while I was gone. Unable to come up with the teacher's name, one little boy assured me, "It was the lady who *used* to own this place."

Room for One More

As my twelve-year-old nephew was about to undergo five hours of delicate surgery, his father couldn't help but notice that, inch by inch, he was scooting toward the edge of his hospital bed. Asked why, he replied, "I'm making room for Jesus."

www.ingramcontent.com/pod-product-compliance
Lightning Source LLC
Chambersburg PA
CBHW072045290426
44110CB00014B/1572